Drugs and Our World

A Drug-Free Kids Book

Gretchen Super
Illustrated by Blanche Sims

TWENTY-FIRST CENTURY BOOKS
FREDERICK, MARYLAND

Published by
Twenty-First Century Books
38 South Market Street
Frederick, Maryland 21701

Printed in the United States of America

10 9 8 7 6 5 4 3 2 1

Library of Congress Cataloging in Publication Data

Super, Gretchen
Drugs and Our World
Illustrated by Blanche Sims

(A Drug-Free Kids Book)
Includes bibliographical references.
Summary: Describes, in simple terms, the harmful
psychological and physical effects of drug usage
and outlines reasons for not using drugs.
1. Drug abuse—Juvenile literature.
2. Drug Abuse—United States—Juvenile literature.
[1. Drug abuse.]
I. Sims, Blanche, ill. II. Title.
III. Series: Drug-Free Kids.
HV5801.S8378   1990
362.29—dc20   90-31119 CIP AC
ISBN 0-941477-88-6

Table of Contents

Chapter 1

The Drug Problem

You have learned about drugs.
You know that some people use drugs.
You know that drugs are a problem.

Drugs are a problem for the people
who use them.
They change the way the body works.
They make people sick.

Drugs change the way the brain works.
They change the way people think.
They change the way people act.
Drugs hurt the people who use them.

But did you know that drugs are a
problem for everyone?

Drugs also hurt people who do not
use them.
Drugs can even hurt you.

"How can drugs hurt me?" you may ask.
"I'm a drug-free kid!"

Drugs can hurt you even
if you don't use them.
What one person does
can hurt everyone.
When people use drugs,
they hurt everyone.

What one person does
can also help everyone.
When people say "No" to drugs,
they help everyone.

This book will show you how drugs
hurt everyone.
It will show you why drugs are a
problem for everyone.

And it will show you why everyone
should say "No" to drugs.

Chapter 2

This Is Our World

This is our world.
And you are a part of it.

There are many different places
in our world.
There are many places for you to see.

There are many different people
in our world.
There are many people for you to meet.

Everyone is a part of our world.

You are a part of your family.
Your family is a part of a neighborhood.
Your neighborhood is a part of a city.

Your city is a part of a state.
Your state is a part of a country.
Your country is a part of our world.

We live in a big
and beautiful world.

And there are many
wonderful things to share.

This is your world, too.
You share the world
with the people you know.
You share the world
with your family and friends.

You also share the world
with people you don't know.
You share the world with everyone.

The world is ours to share.
And it is our job to take care
of the world.
We must keep our world clean.
We must keep our world safe.

You have to do your part to make
our world a clean and safe place.
What you do can help everyone.

Some people are not good at sharing.
Some people do not help to keep
our world clean and safe.

People who use drugs are
not good at sharing.
They don't help to make our world
a clean and safe place.

DRUG-FREE
KIDS

People who use drugs have a problem.
It is a problem that hurts many people.
It is a problem that hurts the world
we share.

Chapter 3

People Who Use Drugs

Why are drugs such a big problem?

Drugs are dangerous to use.
They hurt the people who use them.

Drugs change the way the body works.
They make people sick.
Drugs change the way the brain works.
They change the people who use them.

Drugs change the way people feel.
People who use drugs may feel
upset or angry.
They may feel sad or afraid.

Drugs change the way people act.
People who use drugs may say things
they don't really mean.
They may do things they don't
really want to do.

Sometimes it is very hard for people
to stop using drugs.
They feel sick if they do not use drugs.
They are addicted to drugs.

People who are addicted to drugs care more about drugs than anything else.

They may lie or steal to get more drugs. They may get in trouble with the police. They may stop going to school or work.

People who use drugs hurt
the world we share.
They may no longer think
about other people.
They may no longer care
about other people.

People who use drugs hurt everyone.
They hurt people they don't even know.
They also hurt the people they know
and love.

Chapter 4

Drugs and the Family

Your family is the group of people
you know best.
They are people you love.
They are people who love you.

But drugs change people.
They may change someone
in your family.
They may change someone
you know and love.

It is hard to live with people
who use drugs.
They may be mean to other people.
They may not want to be a part
of the family.

24

If people you know are using drugs,
they may seem like strangers.

You might think
you don't know
them anymore.

You might think
you don't love
them anymore.

If someone in your family is using
drugs, what should you do?

You don't have
to be frightened.

You don't have
to feel alone.

You can find someone to talk to.
You can share this problem
with someone else.

It may be one of your parents.
It may be a teacher or a doctor.
There are many people
who will help you.

People who use drugs need their
families more than ever.
They need love more than ever.
They need help to stop using drugs.

People who use drugs don't want
to hurt other people.
But they do.

Chapter 5

Drugs Hurt Everyone

Drugs hurt the people who use them.
They hurt the families and friends
of the people who use them.

And drugs hurt other people, too.
How can drugs hurt other people?

Let's look at some of the ways.

Driving and Accidents

People who use drugs don't help
to keep our world safe.

People who use drugs cause
many accidents.
They make the world unsafe
for everyone.

Some people use drugs and drive cars.
That is a very dangerous thing to do.

People who use drugs may not
be able to drive safely.
They may not be able to think
quickly and clearly.
They may not be able to stay awake.

People who use drugs cause
many car crashes.
Car crashes hurt and kill many people.
People who use drugs make the roads
unsafe for all of us.

Smoking

People who smoke don't help to keep
our world clean.

You know that tobacco smoke
hurts people.
It hurts the lungs of the people
who use it.
It hurts the hearts of the people
who use it.
It causes a disease called cancer.

Tobacco smoke hurts other people, too.
When you breathe someone else's
smoke, it hurts you.
The smoke makes your throat burn.
The smoke makes your eyes red.
The smoke can make you sick.

People who smoke make
other people sick.
They make the air unclean for all of us.
They hurt the world we share.

Pregnancy

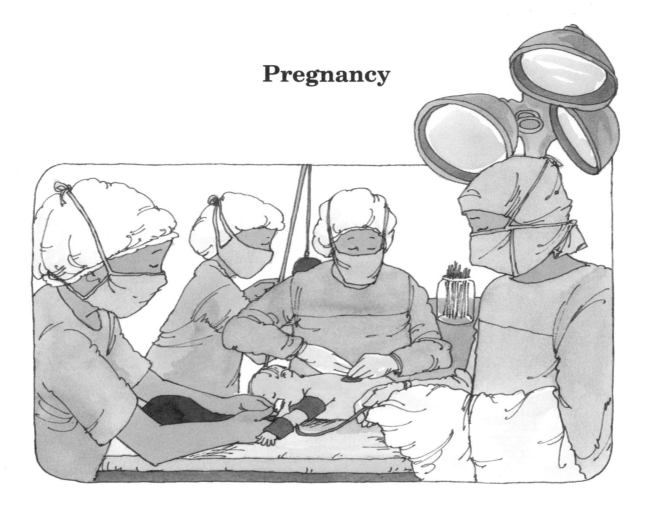

Drugs hurt the bodies of young
people most of all.
Drugs can even hurt babies before
they are born.

When a pregnant woman uses drugs,
the baby inside her can be hurt.
Drugs can make it hard
for an unborn baby to grow.
Drugs can make an unborn baby sick.
They can hurt an unborn baby's
body and brain.

After they are born, these babies get
sick more often than other children.
They may have to stay in the
hospital a long time.

These are some of the ways that
drugs hurt everyone.
These are some of the reasons
why we have laws about drugs.

Chapter 6

The Laws about Drugs

You share your school with other kids.
There are rules to help everyone
get along.
There are rules to keep everyone safe.

We share our world with many people.
There are laws to help us get along.
There are laws to keep everyone safe.

Drugs make our world unsafe.
That's why there are laws
about drugs.
There are laws about drugs to keep
our world safe.

There are many laws about drugs.
But one law is easy to remember:

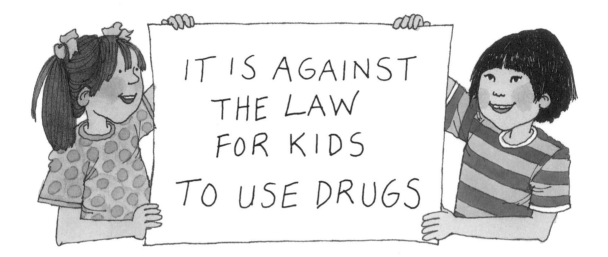

IT IS AGAINST
THE LAW
FOR KIDS
TO USE DRUGS

Kids are not allowed to drink alcohol.
Kids are not allowed to smoke cigarettes.
Kids are not allowed to use
marijuana or cocaine.
Kids are not allowed to use drugs.

Some drugs are against the law
for grown-ups, too.
Marijuana and cocaine are against
the law for everyone.

No one is allowed to use these drugs.
No one is allowed to buy or sell
these drugs.

Some drugs are not against the law
for grown-ups to use.
Grown-ups are allowed to use alcohol
and nicotine.

They can drink beer, wine, and liquor.
They can smoke cigarettes, cigars,
and pipes.

But alcohol and nicotine are not
safe to use.
They can hurt people.
They can hurt our world, too.
That's why there are many laws
about them.

It is against the law to drink
too much and drive.
It is against the law to smoke
in many places.

We have laws to keep our world
safe from drugs.
But not everyone listens to the laws.

Some people do drink and drive.
Some people smoke where they are
not allowed to.
Some people use marijuana or cocaine.
These people are breaking the law.

Breaking the law can get people
in big trouble.
They can even go to jail.

People who break the law hurt
other people, too.
People who use drugs hurt everyone.
That's why everyone should
say "No" to drugs.

42

Chapter 7

Be a Drug-Free Kid

This is your world.

It is a big world.
It is a beautiful world.

You share the world with many people.
You do your part to keep the world
clean and safe.

You are a drug-free kid.
You say "No" to drugs.

Saying "No" to drugs keeps our world
safe for everyone.
Saying "No" to drugs keeps our world
clean for everyone.

When you say
"No" to drugs,
you say "Yes"
to a healthy you.

You say "Yes"
to a happy you.

You say "Yes"
to a smart you.

44

Remember that one person
can help everyone.
Saying "No" to drugs helps
everyone in our world.

Words You Need to Know

Being a drug-free kid is a big job. But you can do it. Knowing about drugs will help you stay drug-free. Here are some words you need to know.

addicted	when someone can't stop using drugs
alcohol	a drug found in drinks like beer and wine
cocaine	a drug that comes from the coca plant
crack	a kind of cocaine that is smoked
drug	something that changes the way the body and brain work
joint	a marijuana cigarette
marijuana	a drug that comes from the cannabis plant
medicine	the kind of drug a doctor gives you when you are sick
nicotine	a drug found in things made from the tobacco plant
peer pressure	when other people make you feel that you have to do something
poison	something that hurts the body if you eat or drink it

Index

Drugs and Our Children

A Note to Parents, Teachers, and Librarians

Drug-Free Kids is a book series for children ages 5 to 8. Our children, even at this early age, hear about drugs, but they may not understand what the drug problem is about. They know that drugs are a problem. But they may not know why or how.

This series was written to help young children understand why and how drugs are a problem. Drug-Free Kids places the problem of drug use within a framework of issues children may already know about—issues such as health and wellness, social responsibility, and personal choice. The need to say "No" to drugs is presented not as a question separate from the other important decisions our children have to face, but as one part of an outlook on life that enables them to grow up happy and healthy.

These books are designed to encourage independent reading. But no book series on drugs can take the place of active adult involvement in the lives of our children. I hope you will take the time to read these books with your children or students. They will have questions, and you may not have all the answers. But Drug-Free Kids gives us an excellent start. It opens a dialogue on one of the most important challenges of our time: how to teach our children to say "No" to drugs.

Lee Dogoloff, Executive Director
American Council for Drug Education